The 2018 Missouri "Show Me the Poetry" Series:

Raphael Maurice / *The Idiot's Calendar*
Brett Underwood / *Mush*
Chigger Matthews / *Rockstar / Paperman / Scissorhand*
Sean Arnold / *Lost and Found by the Muddy Banks*
Jim McGowin / *Murmuration*
Benjamin Kuzemka / *Dance Grooves for Gotikara*
Kevin W. Peery / *Bootlegger's Bluff*
R.C. Patterson / *Black Magic*
Jeanette Powers / *Sparkle Princess vs. Suicidal Phoenix*
G.M.H. Thompson / *Yard Sale at the Devil's Petting Zoo*
Stefene Russell / *47 Incantatory Essays*
Marybeth Niederkorn / *Times Knew Roamin'*

The Cosmic Lost and Found:
An Anthology of Missouri Poets

Edited by Jason Ryberg

Kansas City   Missouri

Spartan Press
Kansas City, Missouri
spartanpresskc.com

Copyright © Jason Ryberg, 2019
First Edition 1 3 5 7 9 10 8 6 4 2
ISBN: 978-1-946642-97-4
LCCN: 2019930189

Design, edits and layout: Jason Ryberg
Author photos: Raphael Maurice, Jim McGowin, Opalina Salas,
Virginia Harold, Lucy Kuzemka, Kevin W. Peery, R.C. Patterson,
Jeanette Powers, Drew Sheafor, Kevin A. Roberts, Kassi Jackson
All rights reserved. No part of this publication may be
reproduced or transmitted in any form or by any means,
electronic or mechanical, including photocopying,
recording or by info retrieval system, without prior
written permission from the author.

This book and the series that it accompanys, encapsulates, summarizes and, ultimately, puts quite a fine point on, was made possible by, and is dedicated to Mark McClane, Tony Hayden and The Osage Arts Community.

CONTENTS

RAPHAEL MAURICE

[An Idiot's Sonnet by the Sea] / 1
[For James Wright] / 2
[Dearest] / 3
[Gatherings] / 4
[Goodwill] / 5
[The Storm] / 6
[This Land Is Your Land] / 7
[Sonnet 59] / 8
[Sonnet 61] / 9
[Sonnet 78] / 10

BRETT UNDERWOOD

December Night / 13
Memories of Father / 15
Only Cannibals Take Heart / 16
The Give and Go / 18
Symphonic Gurgle / 19
Wagon Wheel Cities Are Annoying / 22

CHIGGER MATTHEWS

Chapeau Hollow / 25
cloud watching / 26
tree-winter-sky (or, the Dyson Sphere) / 27
thought experiment / 28
What I Wanted / What I Found / 29
Midwest Flyover / 30

Rural Progressives in My Part of Missouri / 31
Reasons I Keep Quitting Smoking / 32
puzzlement and frustration from oversleeping / 33
See-Saw Riddle / 34

SEAN ARNOLD

Big Jim Plays Shady Grove / 37
Soliloquy From a Freight Yard / 39
For Hemingway / 41
Out Your Way / 42
Mercy and Pain, Pain of Mercy / 43
Poetry Game Huck Finn / 44
Social Services Worker / 45
Purgatory Forest Gump / 46

JIM MCGOWIN

Root / 49
The Folly of Watching for Specific Chromaticity / 52
Muse and Eat Her Too / 54
And Then the Clay Became Like Flesh / 56

BENJAMIN KUZEMKA

I eat Sun Chips when I pray / 61
I only trust a god who remembers / 62
These days I read the Four
   Quartets backward / 63
In love, she was something
  of an Argentinian Nazi / 64

With you, I saw the world never end / 65
It's New Year's Eve at the Hyatt / 66
A weeknight bleeds across the Beltway / 68
A plane overheads, a kitchen light buzzes / 69
In '88 I brought the snow to Manhattan Beach / 70

KEVIN W. PEERY

Hand Grenades at Holy Cross / 73
Poor Man's Pollock / 75
Fried Chicken & Tequila / 77
Shell Pink Stratocaster / 79
Corn Mash Moonshine & Mickey Gilley / 81

R.C. PATTERSON

Somnambulist / 85
Elegy 1 of Erotica Matrix / 86
Trapped Like Mice / 87
What Does It Mean to be a Realist? / 88
The Colony / 89
Nietzche on the Fair Housing Act / 91
Brand Nubian / 93

JEANETTE POWERS

The Cosmic Lost & Found / 97
Keep Your Finds / 100
Casting / 101
Perfectly Good Muses / 103
Agitation / 105

G.M.H. THOMPSON

Airy Anecdote / 109
Strawtrance / 110
True Horror / 111
65 Million Years Ago: / 112
The Death of a Tree / 113
A Butterfly / 114
Havana / 115
The Drunken Bum / 116
Churchyard / 117
Supermarket / 118

STEFENE RUSSELL

Excerpts from The Possum Codex
  (Otis Nebula, 2015): / 121
Three Note Oddity / 130

MARYBETH NIEDERKORN

Highway Thoughts / 133
Vulture / 135
Junction City / 137
The Moon Rocks Over / 138
Stranded / 139
Even the City Has Its Limits / 140
Modesty / 142

*...adrift
amidst these oddments
the keeper of the left behind
the recorder of what's missing...*

-Jeanette Powers

Raphael Maurice

Raphael Maurice is a poet, translator, and teacher. He resides in Washington, MO where the river keeps its secrets.

[An Idiot's Sonnet by the Sea]

With me you walk through brutal days
both of us confined to our separate minds.
While netted, trapped within these crabbed lines,
I thought of you and those nights in which you raged.
As if you'd seen another world that collapsed & lay
at your feet in order to be sorted out by time.
It wasn't so. The errors we had made were blind,
like Homer's catalogue of ships —
undone by the ocean's play —
the sea it claps against the hull,
seawater spits out the bay.
I did not want things to pan out like this,
the hit of water against another boat,
our dreadful, waterlogged days and nights.
It was your drenched naming of each and every kiss.
You'd lean, and lip-to-lip, touch what you had hoped:
and in the drooling night you groped to find
a darker sort of bliss.

[For James Wright]

Miles down the locust road towards town,
at the dusty bar in which years later I will waste
myself on an unhinged, three-year bender—
material for a few fractured songs—
they smoked and drank, the men's speech
turning into the rhetoric of locusts.

With heavy lungs and desiccated throats,
the old voices teem and mutter in my skull,
shames that cut and bore
like saws and splitters, a mill of failure
churning at the river's shore.

The reeking water still summons us back to work.

[Dearest]

My father said today
how beautiful you were
coming out to greet him
the morning's brightness such
your hands lift
your brow to the sun, the sun.

It's very easy here—
The wind kicks over the river,
we drown, bit by bit, into its arms.
We sweat at night in goodness
in the lamp's truth.
I have not come here to be hurt.
I will be hurt.
I offer a heart of flame
to your mouth.
I give it freely
though it is heavy and has burned
my hands.

[Gatherings]

Fresh off a divorce, I wait on good news
that sounds the man-god's impossible birth.
The seasons bell the Christ's
arrival, as I grow hard & dead
in my ticking house of blood, the heart.
What debt do I owe Him, looking down onto a plate
of shrimp while Aunt Mary gripes the little ones
to suffer in their respective corners?
The afternoon dies like a vast complaint.
Such heavy snow. What is left to say?
Here at my brother's warm & Spartan house
some children come, go out of secret rooms.
I step onto the porch for a smoke—
conscious that my lungs are well past the age
of reason. The smell of pine trails me like a shadow.
Mary talks at the kitchen wall, as my brother's
youngest sidles up to her, looks, waits for her
fierce hands to grow slack, slow,
to acknowledge his body, gather him up,
and forget completely what it was
that so upset and bothered her, us.

[Goodwill]

Evenings rustle round the windows of our Goodwill
faces good faces of children – poolfresh – mothers too
a few confused fathers run still
run hands this is guilt free
shopping frightened books & pottery
the shards shirts Taylor Swift is over & over the satellite
radio my heart a busted shoe radio signals my heart
swarms in new blood marry me families
your observable silence here in a firefly town
we grow tender as the bruise last night
I dreamed of you mother lover you— creekfresh
a white dress your hair disturbed in breeze
grackle black black as the sheriff's new Michelins
you walked somehow into me & I was good again going
nowhere.

[The Storm]

Wait it out   purblind   near the bales.

Sit out the deafening   song of dust   then the rain's sea

a gale   quickening   expanse of the anger-crows.

The uproar   rides the lightning-spines

furred blue electric   backs of hysterical horses.

Swollen coveter   crimson howl

demented   water   thief—

leave us our pile   our flood-bones.

Add up the crawling   the cowering   things of earth,

and divide   monster   divide.

[This Land Is Your Land]

After an afternoon driving through
where I grew up – Viper's Lane,
Retirement Road, Holy Family Hill
buried beneath snow,
the hill dotted by black, electric birds,
blurred by sun, dotted by meth –
shacks, near the ditch of dead pups,
places I'd abandoned – and I lie and tell you
that nothing much happened,
nothing like Bobby Hoffman,
the cows masticating, dumb, dumb, dumb,
entering into bruise-colored barns,
a farmer's sudden wave, church suppers
where most went hungry for the Ghost – I am
still here, cold and raving,
eager to tear and torch the leaning
porches, all they seem to mean –
you tell me to calm down. (A day later,
over morning coffee, you'll tell your mother
on the phone you're sad, sad, and might need
a prescription for meds, or impossible,
a vacation far from our histories, and island,
Lexapropolis, something, one true love.)
But now I get out of the car to smoke,
onto the green shoulder,
looking out over the plots and grids
of Gerald, suddenly, breathing the raw air.

[Sonnet 59]

Go, idiot. Roughen what was straight, calm.
Roughen your little poems.
We weren't put here on the threatening lands to please,
not even ourselves.

Forget the agora's madness, its night-shrieks.
Write yourself into your corner,
back into the black corner,
crooked, fenced-in. Pray off the most sacred thing,
which will and will not be called God.

Weep (like me) into your trembling hands,
weep into the mask around your face and throat.
You're the saddest s.o.b. in the cosmos.
But, that is the way we write.
This is the path we must take.

[Sonnet 61]

I'm your jitterbug boy.
I've got all the money.
I bought up all the tobacco in Honduras.
Where the water's filthy,
where fish cough up other fish.
They sustain themselves this way.

I dragged my half-corpse to the water.
I looked out and wanted to drink the surf.
I nearly Van Goughed the breakers coming in and in.
I did.

The water there was lethal.
Without an open mouth prepared to speak,
I could not sing truthfully about the sea.
I could not tell my lies so that they'd be believed.

[Sonnet 78]

In stillness I grope. I search and wait.
During the dawn as the passing day has shrunk,
I feel a mystery lift.

Emptiness of half-heartedness, a frayed rope
between yes or no. Often my head tapped by something.
My sense is that it is good.

I believe it is good, humble, imperfect, embarrassed.

Tapping. Glowing. Refusing to be named.
I cannot believe or not believe.
I sit in the wind-struck orchard here,
unsure what hits, strikes, what sings, what ends.

Gentle hands through my hair.
When all has been reduced to shrugs or knowledge,
I feel the unnamable humming in my ears.

Brett Lars Underwood

Brett Lars Underwood is a bartender and a gadabout who writes, promotes and produces happenings and mishaps in St. Louis. Once upon a time, he co-published a 'zine entitled *Lick My Squaggle Noose, Clam Tick*. He penned Zen koans for *The Riverfront Times* and *St. Louis Magazine* as well as *Curator*. He has performed in back rooms, backyards, ball rooms, barrooms, basements, coffee houses, courtyards, galleries, museums, rock venues and taverns. His verse and riddles have been published by *The Bicycle Review, 52nd City, The Subterranean, Bad Shoe* and included in *Flood Stage: An Anthology of Saint Louis Poets* and *The Gasconade Review presents: 39 Feet And Rising*. He unleashed *Sunlit Insult*, his first chapbook, in 2011 and *Its Bush Lent Subtle Hints* in October, 2013. Spartan Press published his first full-length book, *Mush*, in 2018. He can be reached at brettlarsunderwood@gmail.com

December Night

Most of the leaves are down now,
like the fear of death we swallow
everyday.
It is what unites us.
It is what separates us.

Fascism in the belly of the starving;
they call it self control.
Running from the fear of freedom;
they call it self control.

Knowing that the butt
is aflame
after the failure of journalism
in a cool, stiff rain
under a broken limb
in a foreign forest,

It is nice
to walk the sidewalks
of a broken world
of misspelled verbs
and broken promises.

After a meal
of unscrambled segues
and dog food
amidst the babble
of the diner attendants
and unimaginative dolts
or a view of the wet,
slick streets alive with oil
and broken neon,

It is nice
to walk home
through the corpses
and have a quiet and lonely
wank and fall silently
asleep on a dirty carpet
of comfort knowing
the rent is due.
The seed is spent.
The credit is overdue.
Until the next nightmare
of awakening.

Memories of Father

The dork singled in the mango salad
or a seedless dressing announced by the waiter.
Kim served what must've been the best lush,
her hair luminescent in the pitch
shown the way to the porter's closet.

It must've been the way she
shifted under Kim's weight
flatulent, and hungry for a moon beam
and another shot...another stout.
But he swore he saw his father's face
in her crotch.

Ugh.

Kim plowed ahead.
That's why they call him *determined.*
That motherfucker won't leave him alone.

...and you can't put that in a Father's Day card.
...or can you?

Only Cannibals Take Heart

Perhaps I should take heart
that you even speak to yourself
in that seldom-viewed blog
that I can't seem to find on mornings
when I search for such nothings,
but only cannibals take heart.

Prescribe downtime and contemplation
to figure out this mess and sweep the bunnies
from their corners, but I like their crunchiness
on the souls of my bare feet and downtime
is not about sweeping.

Were I to walk to the answer,
it would only take a month.
I would find you in a dozen faces.
I would find us in trouble again.
I could do it only to distance myself
from whatever future they say
there is...or I could do it for focus.
The capitalists say I have four days free
of extraneous cash and work
to cipher it out.

I shoot you as you shoot me,
but we don't recognize the barbs.
Why just this morning,
I thought it was just another ache or pain.
Rolled over and groaned, nearly breaking
my schwanzstucker off in the process.
Only then did I remember
that I was dreaming about running
after you, west on Magnolia to Kingshighway
and east to Sauget.

The Give and Go

Did you know?
The expeditor was talking to the gumbo
and wouldn't listen to the wisdom
of the andouille when dialysis landed
on the fish ballot.

The chuckleheads took it
as a clue to ignore.
Given their dos and don'ts;
their wills and wont's
and what comes with the donuts
and coffee, they had to question
the regularity of the clouds' offerings.

The diners were oblivious
as the osprey with the arrow in its throat cried.

The give and go.
You came and you went.
You go along. You get along.
But sometimes
you gotta exclaim,
What?!!!

Symphonic Gurgle

Billy made the first attempt
at 4 a.m. wondered
who thought first about the contrast
of the colors of blood and fresh-fallen snow
and gave thanks that some deeper silence
had fallen over the world.

Pulled the line up with no fish
out of black thoughts and fractured
concepts made digital or blip blap

Luckily, death reached him in dreams
after drams and clouds formed majestic thoughts
of smiling soldiers who admitted guilt
of masturbatory attempts at freedom

Blood gurgled in a symphony, sure.
Can't stop that idiocy.

In the end, though, the birds
don't care where they shit.

Stress Less (or a Lightness of Vision)

The almost.
I've got it.
The almost will take the
game most nights.
I'll have another
Then wish I was somewhere
someone else.
No slaphappy dingaling.

It is inevitable.
I know it.
Still,
there's no one to
stop it.
No mopeydope can.
It is hope which tosses
such feelings aside.
Only hope.
We must hope for a better
tomorrow as
human beings...or else.
Or else what?
One will say,
Hope is a crutch.
Hope is an anomaly.

Hope for less ennui.
Then why?
If why,
then how?

An epiphany:
Stress kills.
So don't worry.
Stop watching.

Stop sucking at
the glass tit of fear.
Do.
Listen and act.
That is it.

Wagon Wheel Cities Are Annoying

Ezekiel saw the wheel in the sky
keep on turning saw some window
sniffin', banana baker in the local asshole
system with slutty, unwrapped hamburgers
saw some exclusive Bugs Bunny video
on at least two computers, a television,
in a reflective window pane.
Heard it on a DVD player plugged
into a gaming console. Hid it in a wallet
and a passport with the angels cropped
out by the bigoted, redneck, woodtick,
gun-toting, surly drinking, Frisbee-chucking,
conceal carry, info warrior, hippy,
ultra city yuppie, over concerned gluten
free, suburban refugee, NPR contributing,
pseudo liberal, pseudo conservative, cowardly
impotent assbags, townie friends grasping
at their *gun* like a sitcom creep.

Sister Mary Soda Poppins cooked her tar
in a spoon over a candle.
Nodded off and dreamt about the whole ball
of wax and life with a good, cheap little guy
with asthma and a good heart.
Secretion accretion ejection depletion
osmosis and the thirst.
Lust hunger greed oozing the eternal slop
while Maggot Brain was finishing a swish and a thud
and only caught them running away.

Chigger Matthews

Chigger Matthews is a language artist living in the American Midwest. Hosts the collaborative feature "Free Chigger Matthews Presents," teaches poetry workshops for all ages, and is an artist-in-residence at Osage Arts Community in Belle, MO. He is the chief editor for *The Artifact, Planet Earth's First Global Poetry Newspaper* and his work appears at home and abroad. You may reach him at chiggermatthews@gmail.com

Chapeau Hollow

I am not a person
so when you speak of me
say that I am a hat
with personality

Not a person
just a hat
switching bodies
saying words

A little smoke and shadow
covering a bag of wind
that moves and shakes
fidgets tics tweaks bug-like
bananas undercover overcoat
doppelganger and changeling
a dual present double agent
of two minds

one here

and the other

looooong gone

cloud watching

ghosts of fluffy buffalo
graze over head
in untold number

the shaggy beasts
billow on thinnest air
as wisp and shade

a once great nation

tree-winter-sky (or, the Dyson Sphere)

on the other side
of the theoretical limits
of science
is magic

a quantum computer
produces results
startling predictability

a probability machine tells
[yes
no
maybe
and
or
neither
nor
when
if
then]

an oak tree
in the winter
scratches the sky

thought experiment

I imagine
a wise man once said (probably)
in life
lift with your legs

but imagine if you didn't have legs
how would you lift things?

you could lift with your arms
if you are lucky to have arms
but maybe you are not lucky

maybe you can ask a friend
but maybe you don't have friends
or at least friends with legs
or arms

possibly you could use wheels and ropes and pulleys
and some sort of leverage
with all the strength
in your body

just imagine it — go on take a moment — I'll wait

ok
you can stop imagining now
the wise man
needs you to lift something

What I Wanted / What I Found

What I really want is one more
cup of coffee for the road cause
on a night of heavy drinking
the light beer tastes like water
and I am floating face down
on the concrete sidewalk, sleep-
talking about New Poets New
Prophets New Gods New Heroes
and everything is New except
bullshit, which is always the same
ol' but hey- it makes the flowers grow
and that's, like, beautiful, man.

Midwest Flyover

We got it all
out here, yep
buncha sky

Just look at it
no seriously
look there
it is falling
all around us

And here we
have our feet
on the ground
cause we're practical
doesn't mean our heads
don't touch the clouds

Yaa, here is the very definition
of head-over-heels
of turning the fall
into cartwheels

Rural Progressives in My Part of Missouri

I am one of those
hard workin'
dope smokin'
gun totin'
River-Rat
Democrats
and I'll go
toe-to-toe
with any
hillbilly
redneck
white-trash
Republican't
and all them
high society
haute couture
scum lords
in Hollywood, D.C.
Fox News? Fuh-
I listen to the NPR!
Yup, I tell you what, cuz,
cause this is America —
and these colors don't run!

Reasons I Keep Quitting Smoking
(for Nadia)

I. Light

I know why we smoke.
Let's be honest— it's cool.
I'm a dragon.
You're debonair.
I've taken this little piece of language like a shiny gold coin,
pinched it between my claws and sucked the tar of its
meaning into my lungs.
(Debonair is usually a word used to describe men as
charming or suave, which suits you perfectly, cause you're
such a cute boi and a great dancer.)
And it helps fill the spaces between the places, like to/from,
hither/here, thither/there, fore/yester, and yon/morrow.
They were empty until we filled them with the fog of
forgetfulness
– how many times have we come this way?
What are we doing here?
O yaa – got a light?

puzzlement and frustration from
oversleeping

at the crack of noon
I'm still in bed
rattling the cage of reality
with a wooden head

how could I be so stupid?
dead to the world, asleep
when I could have been
in the teeth of it, alive

I missed coffee club
before the brilliant dawn
the warmth of good work
well done, why do I do this?

finally rolling over
and o-! that's right
there she is
now I remember

See-Saw Riddle

Q: How do you escape a room with no windows or doors with only a table and yourself inside?

A: Through the whole.

1) You see the table.
2) You see what you saw.
3) You take the saw.
4) You saw the table in half.
5) Two halves make a whole.
6) You crawl through the hole.

Sean Arnold

Sean Arnold is a poet, writer and visual artist residing in South Saint Louis, Missouri. He graduated from Webster University in 2015 with a degree in Creative Writing where he was poetry editor of the Green Fuse literary magazine and studied under David Clewell. Arnold is currently pursuing a Master's in Education from Webster University, and his day job is as a community support provider at a mental health agency. Previous published works include a four-part chapbook series called *Soliloquy from a Freight Yard*, which was based around freight yard romanticisms and the glorious confusion of youth. Previous publications include *Big Bridge Magazine* out of Berkley, *The Green Fuse,* and *Crossing the Divide* (an anthology created by St. Louis' poet laureate Michael Castro to promote unity through poetry). Past music credits include providing spoken word for the bands Barely Free and Holy!Holy!Holy!. For the past three years he has run a reading series out of Foam Coffee and Beer on Cherokee St. entitled Sunday Summer Spoken Word series. Arnold is a lover of dusty trails, back-alleys, freight trains, running, good health and bourbon.

Big Jim Plays Shady Grove

I would never tell Jim that washing dishes at the cafe is
   nasty work Jim who stands on the high cold roofs
   and welds the steel siding plates for HVAC units
Taking his eight week work trip to South Dakota during
   this record cold front.
The company he works for, he says, gets rich while they
   say they only
Have two days a week of work for him
So he's behind on electric, behind on gas, and behind on
   the mortgage on the
Expansive wood panelled house by the Mississippi
   where from the river you can see the river
And the smelting plants smoking silos.
He's got the five kids the wife the new baby, the two
   precocious puppies to round the family out
This would be a good spell of work he says
The heartache of necessity though too
Leaving the family stranded in a rural no-man's land
   where the locals sell you meat for twice the
Usual price because you're from out of town
There's no guessing what the HVAC journeymen of
South Dakota are like
He tells me of his last time travelling for work on the
Arkansas-Louisiana border in Texarkana
The two men who got on a knife fight on the roof and

were allowed to come back the next day
His coworker and him standing 150 feet up on the
   scaffolding in the simmering 115 degree heat wave
Jim looks down at the pond below him and says *Shit Red,*
I don't think those are fish down below us, those are damn
   alligators!

He tunes his mandolin while telling me all this,
   what I'm describing to you
Starts playing Shady Grove with the utmost delicacy
Really wailing at the little instrument with his six foot
   five three hundred pound welder's hands
You gotta do what ya gotta
The cold front should let up
South Dakota will be a bit warmer next week
Shady Grove, my darling.

Soliloquy From a Freight Yard

I would ride the rails over there
Taking a running jump
Attaching myself to that huge and slow moving train
 like a barnacle.
I would jump off a couple miles down the line
And walk back to the dorms
Scuffed up from rolling onto the gravel.
I would paint graffiti onto the compartments of those
 boxcars while I rode
Big blue airy tags.
I wanted an escape
Felt the world pushing
My mind filled with trepidation
I thought that if I could free myself from college the
 terror in my consciousness would clear.
I yearned for life *somewhere else.*
I sought a new Big Rock Candy Mountains of the soul.
The rails could woosh me off to some new kind of
American lonely
In the huge sky and deserted industry of Montana
Or famous weird California
Or the eerie rain and pine of Washington
Or across the border to some unfathomable spring
 time chill in Canadian forests Where I could only
 dimly speculate on the names of the trees

Or I could have starved to death like Chris McCandless
Stuck at the end of the line without guide or prayer in
   wide open and heartbreaking Alaska.
I could have shuddered without my medicine in some
   deserted crossroads of rail-lines and never found my
   way back.

I stayed in St. Louis
Fading eventually into the tuck pointed brick and mortar
In a desolate yet strangely alive part of town
Squatting houses and evading arrests
Confused in the dark matter of my brain
But finding contentment as it came.

For Hemingway

Memories of past soldiers and munitions,
  past dog fights, barracudas, couldn't prepare for this;
A hurricane attacks the Florida coast
Folds the violent winds inwards on Key West.
No argument or shotgun blasts at the sky could
Dissuade its path. Still
Your ghost fires a spirited pistol
Into a treacherous storm and a gentle
Word of pause from the prose of scientific fact.

Aftermath settles,
Hemmingway's lone bungalow lies
Low in the rain still
In tact,
Soaked, but alive approaches
A six toed cat.

Out Your Way

The old hills of Ballwin Missouri
The supermarkets and big box stores that dot it
Are about to expire when everything is shipped from
    Amazon.
To be a street photographer and
Single mother, waitress, former small town lady
Gold haired tan creek dweller in such a place.
To have left an hour and half north for a new life to
    wind up in Ballwin.
To watch Community while in community college.
To fall in love with a 30 year old from Tindr
You don't know their background for sure they
Could be anything.

I wonder when I'll commute out to you and
Drink a lemon water, water the cactus
In the corner of a south city room that is new but a
building
100 years old. I have dreams that are as odd to me as
Palmistry to a psychic. I wonder when I'll be
Out your way.

Mercy and Pain, Pain of Mercy

I think of the pain you've caused
The psychic pain of loss
The sexual pain
The pain of the body's ugly organs.

There is a muttering man
Crumpled on his couch
Unable to face the day
Unable to face himself
Unable to face us, his victims
His children, his paranoia, his
Mistress.

That nasty cold I've been fighting all week
My wisdom teeth pushing through the gums of the
   old teeth.
Physician heal thyself
Meta-Physician heal thyself.
I think of the mercy of my body fighting the cold virus.
Saving enough cash to get the teeth yanked and
   sawed out
Living in a city that takes me to the bridge's edge
But won't let me walk over.

I babysit my father and his delusions so
My mom can sit in church
I think of all the mercy
All the mercy on this earth.

Poetry Game Huck Finn

Poetry game Huck Finn
I paddle downriver
Or alongside it in a 2004 Mazda Wagon.
Jay Rock turns to Sam Cook backdropped by
Those auspicious North County brick mansions.
Rooster hits a hash pen speaking of LeBron, Steph Curry
    and minor figures of the game.
We talk about what we know of Riverview, a mixture,
Conflicts we'll never fully actualize.
The silver wagon lurches and threatens its 10th breakdown.
It's Mayday and I have become certain I'm getting a divorce,
The sand of kickball lots, pasta salad and IPAs mixing with
    betrayal.
Jay Rock speaks on painting pictures like Mona Lisa through
    the speakers.
I have a crooked smile, turn on a Pearl Jam CD and we talk
    about all those unwitting men,
Grunge Rock betrayed by Nu Metal betrayed by hipsters who
    think throwback thrash is any better than either.
The smallness of music taste in the face of the cosmos
    of dead love.
I look into the night river and forget
If it's the Missouri or the Mississippi if we're in
St. Charles or Spanish Lake.
I look into the night river
Loving the thought of alternate possibilities
As the defunct amusement park Cementland
Fades into the distance.
We keep moving.

Social Services Worker

Arms swollen from bed bugs, dry
And itching, comes onto the porch in
Her nightie, stating I heard
Where they give you $75, $100 for
Christmas, I haven't heard of that I
Say, she goes upstairs, the guy who told her this,
Affable, only one day of stubble
Leather-faced, high cheekbones,
Track marks and bug bites along his arms
He tells me *She always comin up with*
Information that later gets disproven,
Let's see if she can find that document about
The Christmas money.

In my line of work folks are always wondering
Where the hookup is.
Like manna from heaven
We deliver social service information
Try to help for the holidays.

Purgatory Forest Gump

The white lightning of the burning night
Chills out into a sedate cloud cover
A narrative of black coffee sitting in a vintage warm
 floral mug
Pretentious, artisanal,
Gives way to the muscularity of milk.

I had a vision last night I was a teenager running down
 a dirt road in Kansas over and over
A purgatory Forrest Gump, running across the
 dirt country
Crossing the nation in the 1960s
Crossing a Kansas county
Crossing my imagination.
Then I wake, the day unfolded a sedate burning,
Cloud cover, a delicate cooling mist
My quadriceps of creamer and still
I remember running.

Jim McGowin

Jim McGowin does art but keeps a day job. He has been published in *Chance Operations, The UCity Review, Rusty Truck, The Gasconade Review* and has authored several chapbooks. He lives in St. Louis, MO with his family and two cats.

Root

The head can be a craggy monastery,
and an old monk dragged into the day,
blinking and torn out of crude dimensions,
in the shape of a dead-tree lean,

A thin line of thought and piled fortification,
a few dreams planted in the soil,
just a little too deep to germinate,

A weeping throat, always asking,
urged to become a white flag in a siege.

Eroding the ratio of uncounted steps
with ragged foot, bone on bone,
in an unacquainted direction and
the slow splitting stone, splattering mud,
footprints that will double back,
down a less tricky way.

> *Old,* said the body,
> too old for twists.

Against the calendar of dead months,
the bones of years,
the grime of centuries —

every fist is a trivial accusation,
an unjust reply to the muted breath,
every pointing finger is
dry kindling for the pyre,
burning to feel the ash of reclamation.

> Go, find a tree before it is planted
> and wait for a root to sit on
> and chant —

I am my own non sequitur!

Barren is the artless grasp of fools —
any form carved in haste will splinter.
Embrace the hope of spirited carelessness —
what is empty in the world
is that which is too partial to you.

Earth and clay melt,
suspended in the water,
belying a body of cracks,
under a reflection of the
empty silver stars,
occupied
like a night of scattered insects,
immersive and brief,

Go and be the naked pathfinder
sleeping alone and content in the rift,
the way is unceremonious and unbinding
and easily retraced —

A line of poetry is always a straight one.

The Folly of Watching for Specific Chromaticity

Bleached machines make their cartwheels
across the sky,
resolute billowy coffins, adrift and cryptic,
paradox tinge and shaped of bones.

And the meat on these days is always tough.

The original dream of the original bird
was to ascend only with my two hands,
working in the rectory of distance,
where all the words scribbled on a single day
might echo
like a blasphemous curse in an empty cathedral.

Autumn day's lesson — one hand on a fake heart,
the other hand a specimen of contradiction,
waving to all the incompatible people
and their incompatible faces,

The folly of watching for specific chromaticity.

Blaming love songs for the rupture that spits
sleep in strings of pessimistic replicas,

Wave upon wave, deafening,
an unsuccessful antidote,

a penchant for frustrated eyes,
homesick,
but hardly looking over in that direction.

The eclipse is a farewell for the visionary,

And surrender is the emotion
where a passage aches most fiercely,
the place where revelations forfeit
and blindly spoken pledges
prefer to do their hunting, while in packs —

Hungry, thin-ribbed, and very nimble.

Muse and Eat Her Too

I want to be a disciple of bliss
and an uncivilized cheat,
to seduce my muse
and eat her too,

Supple in contradictions
and all the bribery abounding —
each and every,
voracious and velvet,

And cursed, with this sordid
need to pry away
at what's been padlocked —
the sublime entrapment found
secreted opposite the keyhole,
tightly trove,
Gordian knot,
hoard of glittery mistakes.

Betray to me
a devotional of groanings,
fanatic and consuming
in my inspired torment,
in my adorations for the sinuous,
tangled up in a forbidden solution,
cleverly disguised as doggerel allure,
lest intentions be laid bare
like storm-blown lotus petals
might fall, desperate and subdued,

As blessed little massacres
in stippled ornamental codex,
fitful and then parching,
all bellyaching compulsion
and a throaty thirst for the aftertaste
she promises in her revival tent,
huckster of snake oil and hooch.

I want to affix that beauty's yoke
onto each failing and rising blunder,
get amnesiac drunk on every communion,
ridicule the archaic and then sleep soundly
like an adoring beast, deep in a lair.

O shapely with gnashes and
impatient camouflage,
O elusive possession,
lashing the demands of
the wanton deed roiling
in every hypnotic crest and trough,
every bite mark and welt,

Give me all these blessed little incursions,
swearing eternal devotion to them
over and over again,
Trembling about the hand and finger
reaching for her blemished genuflect,

The most selfish way I can worship
in all of her holy temples.

And Then the Clay Became Like Flesh

You want to create a burden in the bone's marrow.
I want you to be bright and glinting through parting clouds.

While I am sleeping, you are dreaming about murder.
While you are awake, you send inquisitors to my bedroom.

You think existence lies in constantly wringing hands,
and that naturally, this is an occasion I should celebrate.
I think maybe I should celebrate more at funerals.

I want to start from afar and walk closer to a reflection.
You were gifted at birth with a perfect tailored suit
that has already gone out of style and relevance.

Your old age is a guarantee of boredom.

I have already forgotten what I wanted to keep —
it was just a phase, a slipping between two moving gears.
You tried to convince me that each revolution was absolute.

You say this is no time to die of arbitrary geography,
yet you allow the existence of conflicting perspectives.
I believe in the real, thinking of myself as a form
of connection, built over an illusory skeleton.
You erode away the scaffold my ancestors built below me.

You have long finished the short list of things
you believe should be held in reverence.
I am breathless with the struggle to stay true
to even my smallest of obligations.

You have been howling for my death
ever since I found out that
the pulse is not counted with each throb in the wrist,
but in all the still pauses in between,

I have also stopped counting.

You silence all the escaped birds and kill their songs,
saying: their momentum must be made tragic —
how can they be wretched, if they are free to fly away?

You are not the same as air.

I know each bird is a small disaster waiting to happen.
You like to pit them against their servitude to gravity.
I know that the birds are not afraid of your boundaries.
Despite all your stipulations, they will still learn to fly.

I wait for my body to wear thin — to finally empty
my lightened self into the air, more bird-like than man.

Your intentions for me couldn't be more predatory.

You are content to notice when someone is not at home,
to burn everything hard and let the night grieve on.
You are always working in ransoms.
I believe the rarest of people do not die — they go on,
stirring the clouds above us with their breath.

You think the worth of my confession
is somehow less credible when not ghostwritten by you.
I think whoever falls should be allowed a deserved velocity.

You are without the benefit of the next new morning.
The swollen yearning in your heart beats hypnotic,
but asks for a fire of loathing and coerced praise.

I steal from you the silence that will feed me in my afterlife.

Your mouth is the trance, full of dead star ghosts.
My eye reflects their stellar echoes in answer to the void.

I turn the volume of the universe down into a slow breath.
You insist that sound cannot travel through a vacuum.

I see that your assertions have never been more than mud.
You see that I've actually been flesh and blood all this time.

Benjamin Kuzemka

Benjamin Kuzemka grew up in suburban Chicago and studied English at the University of Illinois. After graduation he lived in the industrial heart of China and suburban Nairobi. He went to seminary, left seminary, met a girl, married the girl, and now lives in Saint Louis.

1.

I eat Sun Chips when I pray;
I stare at peeling birches,
the blank screens, the air
conditioning units.

Oh, and yes God answers.
She's no prude when it comes to suggestions.

Juan Cruz was just listening too hard.
Saints are all like that— expecting
God to be a god
and not a tad bored,
vaguely hangry.

2.

I only trust a god who remembers
that I need more than mere salvation,

which like all things
is magnified
by a story, a good clove of garlic,
a magnificent slap on the ass.

My epochs are the most real
and impermanent of things.

I can convince neither
you nor me
of our utter unabstraction.

But do let November come.

3.

These days I read the *Four
Quartets* backward.

I know so well how
a wash machine settles into place.

Most of this world's grandparents
are dead; we play with their bonds
and their ottomans
and gladly never dream.

—

I look at our pumpkins
and the photos of us picking
the pumpkins

and a chubby little squirrel
beckons my wrist,
whispers *again.*

4.

In love, she was something
of an Argentinian Nazi—

upset, unconfused,
no longer a slave to stomach ailments.

She's the reason
I sometimes drink decaf.

She's my chin-up mentor,
my Aunt Lorelai.

—

Sometimes I wonder
if the saints regret as little as I do.

And they only appear to
humans when needed.

That's why I
never heard Gotikara

before
I saw her.

5.

With you, I saw the world never end.

I saw millstones for Oltec dreams,
and coffee mugs with our faces on them.

My roommate won't stop tuning her acoustic
electric. She gave me this

message that's lighter than bird bones—
a Nephite monstrosity made of salmon and stock yields.

She gave me a Borders gift card
There are no words, no rings in the wood.

I still remember the cricket matches in Pune,
the quick alley Kingfishers, the Starbucks in the lobby,

the apocalyptic worries, Sanskrit lessons,
and pull out methods.

I bartered and bartered for that handknit shawl,
and still I didn't pay enough.

In another lifetime
I could've been Jesus' favorite headrest.

Instead, I got kicked out of a cult.

6.

It's New Year's Eve
at the Hyatt.
Everyone

is speaking, even
me when asked to.
They really shouldn't

let the poetry kids
have Christmas
trees. There's
tradition,

mommies and dads,
tonics, praying,
laughter, light,

asymmetry,
balls. They're
screwed, like

a flutist in a
room full of
clocks. The potato

wedges finally
arrive. I apply
my pepper

and can be
the third reverse
alchemist

westward
leaning,
still proceeding

stomping
on bubble wrap
in cars.

7.

A weeknight bleeds across the Beltway.

French gin, drying foreheads,
a half moon and a baseball game.
A belated decade.

It's as if the sorbet's
been dry-cleaned out of the sherry.

All that's left is
some supercritical gunk
and discounted fish oil tablets.

—

I cherish my photos of the church
where the kind folks still humped to
Come Sail Away,
fingering ornery
pistachios and choking back
almost alien tears.

Tip your server, yes. But know that
every distant god is near.

8.

A plane overheads,
a kitchen light buzzes,
but it's sickly

bark which tells
me how
gooey
this age will
be.

The gunk
of a Coachella
recycling bin, the gunk

on the remains
of microwavable tortellini,
my Motrin nervousness

and more Springsteen covers
than Springsteen chords.
We were there after the sun

arguing, relaxing.
I never told you I speak
Telugu.

I never told you
what Veblen
could mean
to a hopeful child.

9.

In '88 I brought
the snow to Manhattan
Beach. I felt

a stranger's jawline
and counted
plastic shards.

It is noon, I'm back
in my favorite
Castro

alley stumping
for Allegra.
No one
told us

how slow and steady
slow and steady
could feel.

No one told us
time really
would be a jetplane,

and there are
things in this state
worth
crying for.

Kevin W. Peery

Americana songwriter and Kansas-City-based storyteller K.W. Peery is the author of five poetry collections: *Tales of a Receding Hairline; Purgatory; Wicked Rhythm; Ozark Howler; Gallatin Gallows*. *Tales of a Receding Hairline* was a semifinalist in the Goodreads Choice Awards – Best in Poetry 2016. Peery is a regular contributor in *Veterans Voices Magazine*. His work is included in the Vincent Van Gogh Anthology *Resurrection of a Sunflower* and the Walsall Poetry Society Anthology, *Diverse Verse II & III*.

Hand Grenades at Holy Cross

The night
ole man
Murphy
got arrested
for attempted
murder...
he had
five *LIVE*
hand grenades...

Stashed
away safe...
in an
organ donor
cooler
he'd swiped
from a
transplant
team at
Holy Cross
Hospital...

And
nobody
on the
South Side....

ever expected
to see...
his long
forgotten
face...
on Channel
2 News
at 9pm

Poor Man's Pollock

At
3 AM...
I had
the need
to see
what a
hydra-shok
could do
to a can
of Allis
Chalmers
orange...
So
I placed
a case
of Krylon...
on the
regatta blue
trunk lid
of my
ex-wife's
87 Ford
T-Bird...
Then let
my six
ninety six
dash two...

Leave
a poor
man's
Pollock...
And
an
I
owe
you

Fried Chicken & Tequila

I
just heard
John Prine say...
the best thing
about recordin'
with Dave Cobb
at RCA...
was the
good fried
chicken
and top
shelf
tequila...
And
I'm really not
that surprised
to hear him
say it...
Because
most of
the best
Americana
scribes...
have come
to realize...

Even
the cheapest
tequila...
and bad
fried chicken...
are better than
dependin'
on a
fad religion...
Or the more
expensive
things...
desperate writers
try to do...
to just
get by

Shell Pink Stratocaster

(For Tony Joe White)

There's
an old
diamondback strap
still attached
to that cracked
shell pink
Stratocaster
he left
on stage
the last time
he played
at Red's Lounge
down in
Clarksdale...

And as
Rich Woman Blues...
bleed warm
straight through...
that ole
Fifty-Seven
Seeburg
in back...

I know
the Swamp Fox
is gone...
but his
spirit
lives on...
in those
songs
that'll move
mountains
forever

Corn Mash Moonshine & Mickey Gilley

(For Grandpa Wayne)

In my
lever action
memory...
I can still
remember
the long
cold Winter
of 88...
When
we took
Dad's Scottsdale
out across
Roach Lake...
Listenin' to
Mickey Gilley
on 8-Track
tape...
While sippin'
corn mash
moonshine...
from an
ole red
seven
bottle...

That Grandpa
had stashed
under the
tattered tan
bench seat
just six
weeks
before

R.C. Patterson

RC Patterson was born and raised in the City of St. Louis. He has a Masters in Philosophy from the University of Missouri-St. Louis and he teaches philosophy at Harris-Stowe State University. He has self-published several books including *Elegies, Black Lives Splatter,* and *Jim CroMagnon Man.* He is currently working on a novel and a short story collection.

Somnambulist

The city got me trapped in somnambulism.
Gods buried children alive.
That's why I had to have the schism
from a rigid idealism to pragmatism.

Pragmatics of my drastic dogmatism transcends
fanaticism.

I lost religion after I witnessed
Paul Ryans privileged privatize twin barrels
drive by Ms Daisy, with Fitzgerald driving drunk.

So I dove into literature.
Got a literary pictionary,
literally speaking daggers.

Causing primitive patriarchs to Shakespeares
Like a Zulu army horrified after watching Macbeth
actresses massacred by a maglev into platters,
let's fast track.
Turning my brand of urban semiotics
into speech acts.

Elegy 1 of Erotica Matrix

Here's where I have planted my garden
whose golden fruits are products of
noumenal experiences in the fifth
dimension. A damsel with dementia
weeps parabolas bleeding from
Polonius, stabbed with polonium
Spears.
Apollo must be balanced!
This is why I left the Matrix
with Morpheus.
The Dionysian
machine rivers wake me up from hypnosis.

Trees are pikes impaling
the earth draining her,
like leeches on a lake of blood.
Clouds are gray canvases
I painted with my eyes.
I painted the green,
but it's winter
The damsel with dementia
followed me.
Now I feel my two-ness.
Split like a pizza.
Dinner for Apollo
and the Dionysian.

Trapped Like Mice

Trapped like mice in high towers.
Invisible red lines keep me from food.
He keeps me from her.
Kept from bread crumbs.
Cut off from love.

Trapped like mice in high towers.
Just waiting to starve, to end this living.
Cut off from friends.
No company in this prison.
Just waiting to starve, alone, so hungry.
Why am I still trapped, you won, you don't need me!

Trapped like mice in high towers.
Red lines get trampled.
Burned up and shattered.
Pushed to revolt, can't keep us from shit.
Pushed to assault these red lines and gatekeepers.
I am free, you lost, I can finally see her!

But she found me beneath the rubble of towers.
Cut off from love, her love grew sour.
Kept from bread crumbs.
Her children starved trapped like mice in high towers.

What Does It Mean to be a Realist?

What does it mean to be a realist?
It means that happiness exists.
Happiness is as real as numbers drifting like fall
foliage creating a collage painting the canvas of my
imagination, because I see love in the faces of people
who fly through life like biplanes.
Nothing is more beautiful than a positive attitude.
An attitude as genuine as my niece when she says

I love you uncle, look what I got you for your birthday.

As she holds a notebook with several strips of paper
haphazardly glued to the cover.
I refuse to tell her that it's not my birthday.
But this is that honesty that I seek to be like.
Honesty is also real.
Love is real.
This is what it means to be a realist.

The Colony

Wealthy religious right run All the State.
Draining resources leaving me dehydrated
because I drink the dusty blood of the so called
great men. I rehydrate off the teat of mother
Africa milking wisdom from slain empires.

Mother Africa gives!

Europe takes from American colonies on
dusty roads, smugglers, thieves,
early American hustlers
live under British restrictions.
No rights, no time to feel sorry,
so they revolt.
They empty ships full of tea,
representations of colonial oppression.

This is after years of oppression,
soldiers shooting civilians.
Bullets hit you in the heart,
making you willing to kill.

Sitting in that apartment,
next to the glock.
Got a headache,
the room is tenebrous.

Cops barge in.
You point the pistol
because they ain't announce shit.
Folks trapped in the colony.

In an instant the colonialists took away
the second amendment.
Bleeding out on the floor.
Cops run up and take guns.
Colonial cops kill babies.
Politicians speak openly about loathing niggas.
In the colony Jefferson City offers no apologies.
They just ask for more colonial cops.
Needed resources from Johannesburg to
Jennings are restricted by the imperialist.

City politicians talking unity, but I ain't impressed
with your white savior complexes.

Black alderman with a grip on all the sexist sins.
Couldn't come together once
to fight the colonialists.

These are just some thoughts as
I chill out at the pub, the brewery,
the bar.
Put some change in the machine,
play some Jay, some Future, some Nas.

Nietzche on the Fair Housing Act

the out-migration of middle
and working-class families
after the passing of the Fair Housing Act
during this Civil Rights Movement
which left the remaining poor
with strained neighborhood institutions
and reduced access to job networks,
and absolutely no leaders no higher men.

The need of nationalism
to hate those who are different pushed
the white populations and industries
out of the inner city.

As the Rust-Belt died the Sun-Belt expanded.
You can go too far with A Pathos of Distance
you can go too far leaving people
in a miserable state.

People need strong leaders
and they need to become strong leaders.
Thus leaders, who are strong have a responsibility
to the powerless.
Although much of the underlying economic
and social disorder fuels intergroup conflict,

*Human relations will not improve in a vacuum;
real changes must occur to improve
the lives of people.*
The inner city needs improved community
access to capital,

jobs and better access to employment
opportunities,
an improved educational system.

The worst thing to happen to the inner city was
the loss of its nobility.

Brand Nubian

Introducing
Brand Nubian Nirvana
sipping, guzzling Stag.
Trying to drown out trauma.
Stationary as a vacant stare he's
been placed there by feet weary
from chasing nightmares.

I came here for convivial diverting enjoyment.

I'm trying to stop whining and stop lying.
Too much to be proud of.
New young musicians singing.
Fuck the bullshit,
this towns a musical melting pot.
Individuals mixing,
moving to new music.
Young physicians selling pot.
Me and my cousins went to his crib
Bumping,
blasting bombastic beautiful sexist tunes.
Went back to their crib.
Making music with them
where music lives.
Music vivid as livid
Christians preaching
from pulpits on street corners.

They bought some weed and drove
from Ferguson to Berkeley.
The night was caliginous
as prosecutorial sentences.
Thinking about these police, hurting free
beings on the border
of being and not being.
In their small white house
the beat was dropped,
like youthful fantasies of thick models.
Dropping assets,
like criminals fleeing a trap house,
the beat was an auditory light house.

I came here for convivial diverting enjoyment.

Employing this ecstasy,
this hash to repress me as I relax chatting.
Thinking about the party at the apartment I'm in.
I raid the fridge and stoke my fire with the
depressant, beer.
They had the reefer out,
I brought the liquor we were loud.

Jeanette Powers

Jeanette Powers is a painter and poet-writer living on the banks of the Gasconade in Belle, Missouri with her hound dog, Ollymas. She is the author of five full-length books of poetry and numerous chapbooks and has been featured in online and print magazines such as *Trailer Park Quarterly, Ghost City Review,* and *Thimble Lit Magazine.* She is the founding editor of Stubborn Mule Press and a board member for the Kansas city-based poetry festival, Fountain Verse. jeanettepowers.com @novel_cliche

The Cosmic Lost & Found

If there's a cosmic lost and found
and you know where to find it
then you know where I'll be
heaped on top of a pile
of discarded whatevers
lost gloves
and scarves and hats
an inexplicable bathrobe
a number of solo socks
your copy of the Tao te Ching
by Ursula le Guin
the necklace you stole
from your mother
that reminded her
of your father
the keys to the lock
on your glovebox
but not whatever
is trapped in there.

I'm sifting through both
things utterly forgotten and things
that plague you with the nagging
question of where you left them.

I sit on an infinity of bobby pins
and rubber bands
the frame containing
all but the senior year photos
of your son, even the one
where he wore the aubergine beret
there's your ring in the shape
of a leaping horse Nicki lost
there's the leather belt you tooled
in 8th grade shop class with the letters
R O Y, for your grandfather
centered between filigrees
on my lap is the white cat
that ran away one spring
who had white eyes and a fat belly
lying with his head on my knee
is your golden retriever
which your step-father sold
for killing the grass along the fence-line
where he ran and ran.

My bed is made of all the junk mail
never read and never missed
and notebooks lost with only
a few front pages filled with
the insecure marks of hesitant youth
somewhere around here
is your first Danzig cassette

that Bob Dylan poster
and the tape with your father's voice
which you never did listen to
all the way through
because it made you cry so hard.

There I am adrift
amidst these oddments
the keeper of the left behind
the recorder of what's missing.

There's me whistling
a little tune
you made up
when you were nine
about the clouds
and the horses.

There's me
waiting to be found.

Keep Your Finds

On the ground:
    a rosary.

She thinks:
    no one left this deliberately.

There's a difference between
being lost and being litter.

Was it thrown off in a fit of anger:
    because suddenly God was lost?

Was it dropped in a rush to help a friend:
    because prayers suddenly weren't enough?

In her hands:
    a rosary.

She thinks:
    here is life's great mystery.

We're always wondering
where we came from and why.

We're always left curious
about who lost what and how.

Casting

A casting
is an assignment
of a person to a part
an envelopment
of a broken bone
in the precise way
it must heal
an original sculpture
to be copied
for the masses.

A casting
is when
a fishing reel
mounted with bait
is sent flying
to the lake
with hope
of a catch.

A casting
is a way
of asking
questions
so as to
catch a compliment

of way of clothing bodies
to make mummies
which survive
time's decay
and what all of this
teaches me

is that this casting
about for words
to describe
some metaphor
is rich in history
that anyone
may play the part
set the bone
make the bust
fling the reel
be made
to feel beautiful
and maybe
be cast
into something
worth
dying
for.

Perfectly Good Muses

I'm not on speaking terms
with a single one of my muses
and that's what keeps me writing these days.

They're still perfectly good muses
every poem is a puzzle box, a bottled ship
a sand dollar or locked vault or riddle
I'm hoping gets solved or shattered
or shared with my affections.

I'm not on speaking terms with a single one
of them, much as I love silly putty and snow globes
much as I love pickles and whiskey and roots
much as I love musing about amused muses
but there is a line between being captivating
and being held captive.

But we did roll our eyes so good together
back in the day before we knew our worth
(before we knew our price)
back when they graced me
with their gated community flair.

It turns out the critical part of a muse lives on
in the absence of the physical part of one
muses keep renewing their lease in the head

and I go about my business
of flat-lining life on the page.

I put a real pin in it
. . .
muses are beyond all this
this is all beneath them
and they are about the better business of being.

Agitation

@&#^$%
is building frustration
a house of squinting eyes
and worry lines
crossing the face
the world
invading your space
control
faltering
      tectonically
beneath your feet
just before you're grasping
at the broken glass
where the windows
gave way.

Brute momentum
reverberating through your home
and the mounting rage
of treasures taken away
you're shaken and
it's as if someone's
hit the repeat button
on your worst conceptions
the earthquake lasts
a moment
but the agitation remains.

Days, weeks, decades
the anger abides
and cascades
into corners of your mind
long dormant
the dust rising from the basement
the stench of skeletons
fresh again
you can't shake
the wrong done
it shows from the cracks
in the walls
to the pinched lines
between your eyebrows.

Until you can't tell
anyone
whether it's you
or the house
that crumbled
or
which is the damaged goods.

G.M.H. Thompson

G.M.H. Thompson was born on February 15th, 1990, at about 12 midnight, in a hospital in Cleveland, Ohio.

Airy Anecdote

—Did you hear about the balloon
    that got away?
It had a tether
      I don't know why
  & wherever it went
        it wrecked.
    The power lines it wrecked.
    The telephone wires it wrecked
    the t.v. towers it wrecked.
Many
thousands of people
were without electricity
& I think finally
they shot it down.

Strawtrance

    emptiness
    corn field
    suicidal:
        strange transformation:
            scarecrow

True Horror

    no one ever sees
   the monster entirely
    out in the open
     and under the bed
     there is only
          a handful of dust

65 Million Years Ago:

Mais ou sont les neiges d'antan?
– François Villon, Le Testament, 336

Only bones remain
& petrified forests
& black seas in our automobiles

Today is a day of sacred ignorance
        a day of jejune decadence
        a day of blind ruination

We each & every one of us is lost
                in forests of ruins
                forests of decay
                forests of sand & ashes
                forests where we are weeping
and know not why

Millennia are grinding to dust all around us
worlds disintegrating in the acid of our unbelief
universes torn to tatters through crass indifference
& there will be no redemption or reparation or
        reawakening.

The Death of a Tree

Thunder came & shivered the tree to deadwood— :
no one came to bury its shattered carcass
which became a playground to hordes of squirrels
climbing the dead boughs.

Grass grew thick to mourn for this fallen titan;—
no one thought to mow its laments to clippings,
making alley cats & raccoons a jungle
kingdom of downfall.

Garbage slept beside this enchanted forest;—
no one tried to throw it away for eons,—
ancient refuse carelessly littered by the
previous owners.

Empty doors stare blind at the broken body— :
no one lives here anymore— no one lives here

A Butterfly

        A pale green,
pale white
          butterfly
   flutters
       timidly
in the wind,
       seeming at certain times
                   & in certain
                          places
        in the course of this
                idiotic
      song & dance number

to resemble a makeshift flag of truce,
a pitiful handkerchief stained pale green
by the puke of the brave captain who was
                    taken

from this world by a stray shell-fragment just
seven minutes, fifty-two seconds beforehand,

leaving his men in
        shocked
            disarray
& greatly facilitating
the subsequent
       surrender
             of the company.

Havana

    a burning eye
      wanders from the window
        yet sees nothing:
          a hand dreams on the sill
            in the tropical night, fondling a cigar

The Drunken Bum

        garbled profanities:
          the Tower of Babel
            both rising & slain,—
       the gesticulating voice
of the mad and homeless night

Churchyard

      fuchsia waves,
   surf ivory:
         Botticelli's shell,
               fallen petals three

Supermarket

    death
            dreams among bananas:
        the Brazilian wandering spider

Stefene Russell

Stefene Russell is a poet and arts journalist in St.Louis, and the 2018 Laumeier Sculpture Park poet-in-residence. Her books include *Inferna* (2012, Intagliata Press), *The Possum Codex* (2015, Otis Nebula) and *47 Incantatory Essays* (2018, forthcoming, Spartan Press). Find out what she did last summer by reading her very sporadically updated blog at stefenerussell.com.

Excerpts from The Possum Codex
(Otis Nebula, 2015):

I fled to the corner
of Axis and Mundi,

in my conjuring city
of sleazy humid
river bars
and dredge barges,

city of painted river walls
and burial mounds,

a half-assed
haruspex at
every butcher counter—

The arpens long-gone,
the apiaries empty,
The streets filled
with miserables
shivering with
dementia a potu
like palsied prairie clover.

Taxis bounce
over busted pavement
and fading Toynbee Tiles:

House of Hades
Colossus of Roads
The Ground Bones
of Dead Journalists.

This town's a haunted
waiting room,
stories hidden
in the names
of its streets,

Numbers painted over
La Rue des Granges
and Rue de l'Eglise.

There's a cop bar
called The Billy Club,
a barbecue joint
called The Lion's Share,

A goose bone prophet
with a horse in his garage,
who canters down Hebert
looking finer than
any sap with a Chrysler.

Even on Tuesdays,
we're all at the tavern—
Yellow beer flows
and fat rogues holler

over the din of the jukebox:
He don't know an asp
from a hole in the ground,

or his own arrogant ass
from hic superbum!

We love to dance
to worn-out records,
the skip and warble
of warping vinyl.

We drop our wooden
nickels in the Rock-Ola,
waiting for the needle to drop

on The New Arcady Stomp,
The Cicada Sisters' one and
only number-one hit.

\#

Bicycling at night
through Carondelet
past The Little Bar
and Kicker's Corner,
and the factory where
they build propellers,

I see curlicues on
green and yellow panels:
factory's stained glass
pocked with
chemical filigree.

Black fragments sparkle
in a metal crucible,
soot blowing off the
coke work's grounds,
making a coalfield of
every brownfield.

My red handkerchief
caught on razor wire.
Syngas blows down Ivory,
down Courtois,
giving us greasy coughs
and coating the windchimes.

No longer Vide Poche
but still filled with empty pockets,
the cabriolets made way
for toughs in Camaros.

Under a pine tree across
from the convent,
I balance my bike
between my knees, screw
open my Thermos,

Toast the night bird
perched on a streetlight
scratching his face
with an orange claw.

Last night, I watched him
perch on the D of
the dollar store, head snug
under one oily wing.

I've got no canary,
and no coal mine.
Just refineries weeping
flame jets, birds circling
the riverfront granaries.

I'm taking the auspices
where I can find them.

\#

In an old pokeberry church
on North Broadway,
the Reverend Dithyramb
belts out an Orphic lecture
on tilth and filth
from a battered blonde dais,

wearing a gold tie
printed with instructions
on how to navigate
the afterlife.

He tells us how a persimmon is a
small orange heart
with pictures inside
describing the weather,
or what we'll have to do
about the weather.

The spoon, for heavy snow.
The fork, for light snow.
The knife, for cutting winds.
A fruit that knows three
words for winter. Three
seed pictures, a way
of talking itself through till spring.

Or else we humans, as
we always do, have reduced
its tongue to near nothing, to signs
that point toward what matters
most to us.

He says, who says persimmons
just talk blandly about the weather?
A spoon could be a flood. A fork,
the devil. A knife, death.

\#

Up at the creaky pulpit,
the Rev thumbs through
a thrift-store reference book,
looking for the directions
to his favorite exorcism.

He's versed in peepstones,
has a madstone for your rabies.
Says eggs carried in a man's felt
hat always hatch as roosters.

I sit in a folding metal chair,
red yarn tied in a bow
around my neck.

Everyone here can smell
some spirit's coppery,
carbonated breath.

Last Sunday, during coffee,
my neighbor's mother
hollered for everyone to gather.
In her pink-gloved hand,
She held out the black receiver

of the pay phone in the foyer:
a terribly wrong number. A
wall of static and purling,

punctuated with creepy whispers,
dogs barking, ear-splitting whistles.
Ghost stories on the party line.

Into the booth our Rev went,
sweaty, hanky to his forehead,
finger-signing three sevens
over his chest. Now listen,

O you sons and daughters of Earth
and starry heaven, he said. Don't make
me dial O for Operator, call up Big O
to sing his hymns—he moves
stones with high pitches,
plucks thunder and lighting
like strings, and totally knows how
to banish the dead.

Three Note Oddity

The android recites it, bright tones on spy radio.
And music: tinny green jazz, fern spores.
The doomed snoop beating the pay phone
with a cheap, unpoisoned umbrella. Dust
after the nail bomb, the dumb alleyway escape,
Vowels in the mouth, dialogue written in clue spray.
The spotter grabs a single hair with tiny tweezers
while passing the table. Hallucinogens baked into
pale blue cupcakes. Blue on blue, no pulse, he's a corpse.
Dead letter drop. Every hour, a pewter voice calls numbers
and the plot of the dope book is weather and death.
Our evaporating dictionary, a wilderness of mirrors.

Marybeth Niederkorn

Marybeth Niederkorn is a reporter for the Southeast Missourian newspaper in Cape Girardeau, and her fiction and poetry have appeared in *Trailer Park Quarterly, Small Town Tales anthology from Kapuha Press, Red Fez Entertainment,* and others. She holds a bachelor's degree in philosophy and a master's in professional writing from Southeast Missouri State University. She lives in southeast Missouri with her husband.

Highway Thoughts
for Dave, my awesome husband

I fell in love with you
in the spaces between.
I think about that a lot,
on the road, where I see
your face in every green
leaf, your heart in every
tree trunk, your eyes
in every space of sky
between the clouds.

I fell in love with you
where life happens.

I fell in love with you
where the lonely places
weren't lonely anymore.

We say fell in love. Like
a tree, a harvested animal,
a successful hunt. Mown
down. But you and I, we
weren't like that. We grew,
from within, an acorn
splitting a boulder
as it rooted and spread.

That's not exactly what I mean.

But love is the building of
a language, and the expression,
a language that hums instead
of speaks. No wonder I resisted.
Words have always meant more
than music, to me.
                        And yet I dance.

You remind me why.

Vulture

It's hard to like a scavenger.
His finery isn't streamlined, his
feet are stained in shades of offal.
It's altogether off-putting, where a
predator stares keenly into you, sees
prey worth attaining, worth pursuing.
Scavengers are ungainly, ragged things,
flopping about, searching, seeking, never
quite getting the laser-beam stare perfected.
But when morning sun catches them
soaring, lights their broken edges
afire, for a moment, just one
fleeting moment, stench
of death evaporates,
the hate the world
bears for them
slips away,
and what's
left could
almost,
almost
be exactly
what's
needed.

Also, vultures
use projectile
vomiting to
get others
to leave
them
alone,
and I
can get
behind
that.

Junction City

I have never felt more as though I am
a dolphin in a redneck tuna net
as when I drive through this place
and see the signs casting about
for customers, none of whom
are me. It kills me.
I do not want to drive down a
somehow-dark-in-broad-daylight alley
at the beckoning of a hand-painted sign
for *Live Bait*.
I can't vote for any of these local
politicians. I would, of course,
vote for Wayne Spain, as his name
rhymes, though it isn't spelled
the way I would've spelled it.
Also,
I don't need an auction company,
or a backyard shed,
or even a stop at Hardee's
only 39 miles from home.

The Moon Rocks Over

The hillside's dewy tonight, and cold
while the moon rocks over us all. I haven't
seen the stars so sharp as they are tonight
in years. It's as though they're seeing me
as much as I'm seeing them, with new clarity,
which is a touch unsettling, to speak truth on
the subject.

But the moon rocks over us all
and softens imperfections daylight seems
to revel in revealing. I could watch it do its
thing for hours on end, never once looking away,
which is the biggest advantage the moon has
over the sun, in my estimation, though the night
has appeals beyond the soft moon and diamond-
bright stars, they shine while the moon rocks
over us all. The cattle low and grasses rustle while
I drive by, watching, thinking. It's how I do, long hours
feel slower, long thoughts go deeper, and I feel myself
pulling into the hillside almost as much as it's pulling
into me while the moon rocks over us all.

Stranded

I don't know why there's a beauty standard what
says long blonde hair is desirable on a woman,
because for me, it's a never-ending parade
through golden spiderwebs, a continual
state of disheveled dress, as I pull fine strands
of burnt-gold filament from my clothing, chairs,
pillows, really anything I graze by
with even an iota of static electric charge.

I realize it's probably not science to think
my hair is attracted to fabric because fabric
holds a charge, slim along the surface, a
charge that doesn't gather and spark unless
someone who's averse to haircuts
wanders past, shedding and unaware.

Even the City Has Its Limits

I keep thinking I'll see changes closer to
the edge, the way I see changes in myself
when I'm close to my own limits, but mine
are not defined by population or property
lines, taxation, voter rolls or anything like that.

Houses sit farther apart, out here, ditches'
weeds are taller, and the road signs are more
likely to be in code, letter and number names,
than named for someone, something.

Once I saw a stray chicken out here, its feathers
green and russet. Reminded me of an oil slick on
a mud puddle. Mud's red here, you know. Some
say it's the iron content in the soil, but since this
up here is in the lead belt, I'd say it's the blood of
broken dreams.

My limits are more about snapping, about the
length between my angry breaths, the distance
from one to ten as I count it out to keep from
screaming, or to keep my blood pressure spikes
in check against the migraine blossom igniting
like so much lighter fluid poured against my skull.

Of course, if the city had migraines, they would probably not manifest quite the same way. Lights flashing in the periphery, crippling pain pressing all activity down, down, until it's not possible anymore—that feels more like an upward limit than an outward one.

Modesty

I think it's weird how Bugs Bunny
walks around naked all the time, but
as soon as he's in drag, he's suddenly
Captain Modesty when a clothing piece
falls off. I like to think this is a scathing
critique of the different expectations of
men and women, in our society, but I'm
not altogether sure that's what's going on
there. I think maybe he's just getting
really into his role—that modesty
exists within women's clothing,
I guess. It's hard to know with
cartoon rabbits.

This project was made possible, in part, by generous support from the Osage Arts Community.

Osage Arts Community provides temporary time, space and support for the creation of new artistic works in a retreat format, serving creative people of all kinds — visual artists, composers, poets, fiction and nonfiction writers. Located on a 152-acre farm in an isolated rural mountainside setting in Central Missouri and bordered by ¾ of a mile of the Gasconade River, OAC provides residencies to those working alone, as well as welcoming collaborative teams, offering living space and workspace in a country environment to emerging and mid-career artists. For more information, visit us at www.osageac.org

HIPPARQUE A L'OBSERVATOIRE D'ALEXANDRIE

www.ingramcontent.com/pod-product-compliance
Lightning Source LLC
Chambersburg PA
CBHW030116100526
44591CB00009B/415